The Nature Kid's Guide to
PANGOLINS

DAVID ANDERSON

LP Media Inc. Publishing
Text copyright © 2026 by LP Media Inc.
All rights reserved.

For information address LP Media Inc. Publishing,
30012 Variolite St NW, Princeton MN 55371
www.lpmedia.org

Publication Data

Pangolins
The Nature Kid's Guide to Pangolins — First edition.

Summary: "Learn all about Pangolins, the Nature Kid Way"
— Provided by publisher.

ISBN: 979-8-89818-178-9

[1. Pangolins – Non-Fiction] I. Title.

Title: The Nature Kid's Guide to Pangolins

CONTENTS

Forest Floors 4

World Wanderers 6

Small Scales 8

Scaly Suits 10

Super Sniffers 12

Armor Up 14

Ant Appetite 16

Tongue Tricks 18

Prowling Predators 20

Roll Up 22

Waddle Walk 24

Night Shift 26

Solo Strollers 28

Finding Friends 30

Precious Pangopups 32

Piggyback Rides 34

Poaching Problems 36

Saving Scales 38

FOREST FLOORS

Crunch! A Sunda pangolin shuffles through crispy forest leaves.

Pangolins live in warm places in Africa and Asia. Some make homes in thick forests. Others live in open grasslands. They rest in dens or inside hollow trees.

The forest floor is a busy place. Leaves and bark cover the ground. Tiny bugs crawl under every log and stone.

Sunda pangolins love shady rain forests. Tall trees and soft soil make a cozy home. These shy animals feel safest in the dark woods.

WORLD WANDERERS

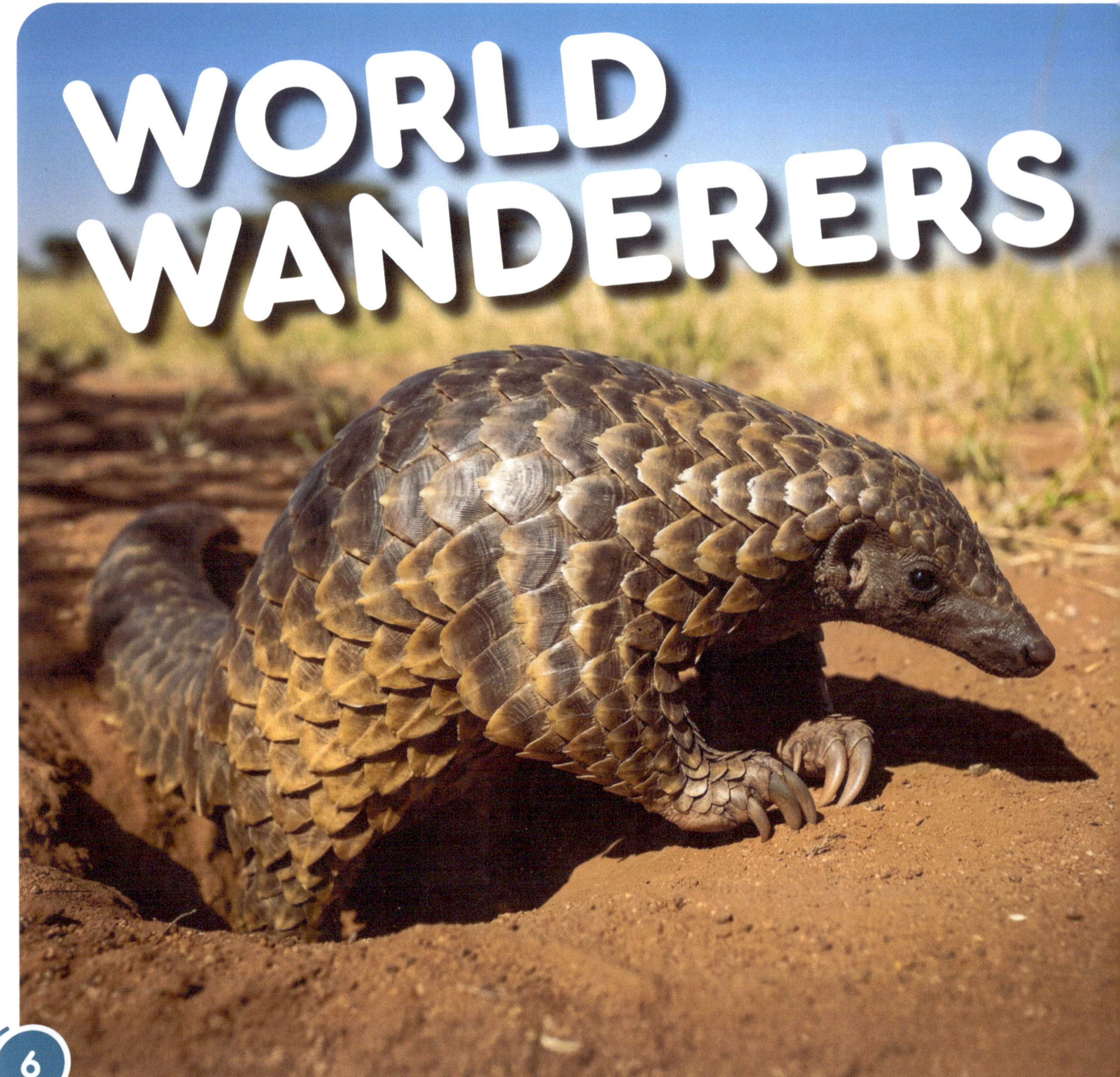

Rustle! An African pangolin peeks out from a burrow in the hot sun.

Pangolins live on two continents — Africa and Asia. Four kinds live in Africa. Four more live in Asia. That is eight kinds in all!

African pangolins roam forests and dry plains. Asian pangolins live in jungles and on rocky hills. Each kind has its own special home.

Indian pangolins live in Sri Lanka and India. They like warm, dry land with loose soil. Every kind of pangolin needs plenty of bugs nearby.

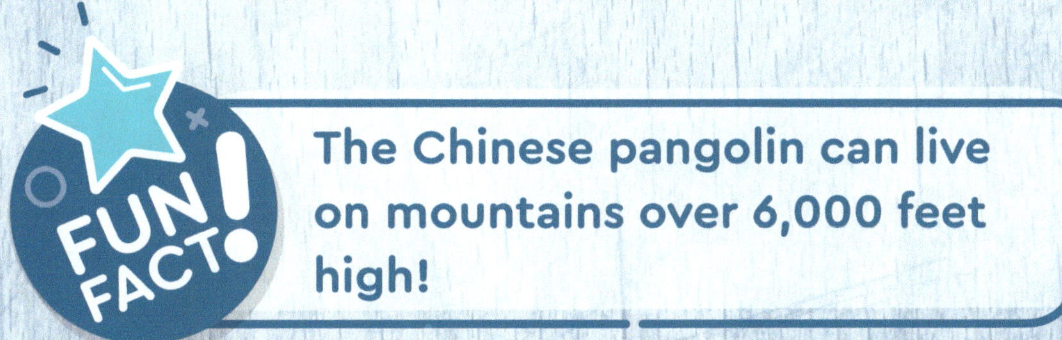

SMALL SCALES

Tap tap! A black-bellied pangolin crawls up a researcher's arm!

Pangolins come in many sizes. The smallest is the black-bellied pangolin. It only weighs about three pounds, as light as a small bag of flour!

The biggest is the giant pangolin. It can weigh up to 75 pounds. That is as heavy as a big dog!

But its tough body makes up for its small size. A pangolin can grip a tree branch so tightly with its tail that even a grown man cannot pull it off!

A pangolin's tail can be as long as or even longer than its body!

SCALY SUITS

DID YOU KNOW?
Pangolins are the only mammals in the whole world covered in scales!

Clink! Hard scales tap together as a Chinese pangolin climbs a tree.

A pangolin's body is covered in tough scales. The scales are made of keratin. That is the same stuff as your fingernails! They cover the back, sides, tail, and legs.

Pangolins have fur on their bellies, not under their scales. The face, inner legs, and belly have no scales. It also has tiny ears and a pointed snout.

Chinese pangolins have smaller scales than Indian pangolins. Each one overlaps the next like shingles on a roof. The pattern looks amazing up close.

SUPER SNIFFERS
FUN FACT!
A pangolin's brain has a huge area just for its sense of smell!

Sniff sniff! A pangolin follows a scent trail in the dark.

Pangolins have an amazing sense of smell. Their noses can sniff out bugs hiding deep underground. One good sniff can lead them right to a hidden ant nest.

Pangolins cannot see very well. Their eyes are small and weak. But that is okay, their nose does most of the work!

Temminck's pangolins do not even have outside ears – just small holes on the sides of their head. But they can still hear just fine.

Between a super-powered nose and sharp hearing, a pangolin has everything it needs to find its next meal.

ARMOR UP

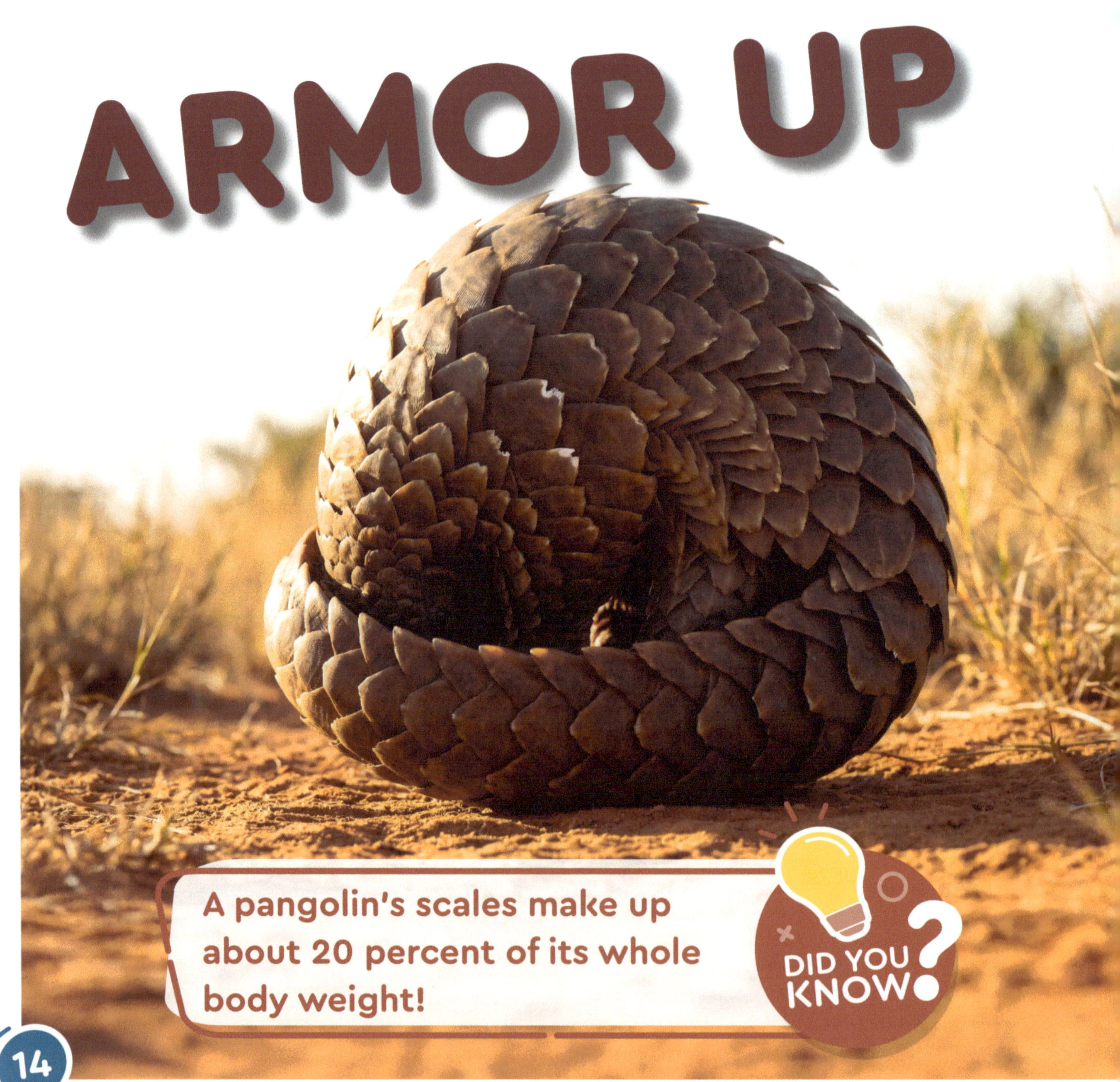

A pangolin's scales make up about 20 percent of its whole body weight!

Wrap! A predator comes close. The pangolin curls into a ball of scales!

A pangolin's scales are its best protection. They are thick, sharp, and very strong. The edges of the scales are like tiny blades. Even large predators like lions and hyenas have a hard time getting through a pangolin's armor.

New scales grow in when old ones wear down. A pangolin can have over 1,000 scales on its body. They fit together to cover almost every inch.

If a pangolin's scale gets dented in a fight, it can fix itself. When the scale gets wet, the dent pops right back out in just a few minutes, good as new! No other animal armor can do that.

ANT
APPETITE
16

Crack! A pangolin rips open a termite mound and starts to feast.

Termites and ants are a pangolin's favorite foods, and just about the only things they eat! A single pangolin can gobble up more than 200,000 insects in one day. That makes them one of nature's best pest controllers.

Pangolins do not chew their food. They have no teeth at all! Instead, they use their long, sticky tongue to slurp up bugs and swallow them whole.

One pangolin can eat more than 70 million insects in a single year!

TONGUE TRICKS

Slurp! A sticky tongue zips in and out of a tiny ant tunnel.

A pangolin catches food with its tongue. The tongue is long and covered in sticky goo. It shoots out fast and grabs bugs in a flash!

The tongue does not start in the mouth. It goes all the way back to the chest! When not in use, it coils up inside the body like a spring.

Giant pangolins have the longest tongues of all. Their tongues can stretch up to 16 inches long.

A pangolin can close its nose shut to keep bugs from crawling in!

PROWLING PREDATORS

Growl! A pangolin hears a leopard. He runs to hide in the bushes!

Pangolins face many dangers in the wild. Lions, leopards, and hyenas all hunt them. Big snakes like pythons try to catch them too.

Hawks and eagles swoop down from above. Baby pangolins are in the most danger. They are small and can be easy to grab.

When a mother senses trouble, she wraps her body around her baby and curls into a ball, shielding it inside her armor like a living safe.

ROLL UP

A pangolin can stay curled in a ball for hours without getting tired!

Whoosh! An Indian pangolin curls into a tight ball in one second.

When a pangolin is scared, it rolls into a ball. It tucks its head under its long tail. Then it pulls its scales tight. Now nothing can get in!

Strong muscles hold the pangolin shut. No animal can pull it open. All those tough scales point out like little thorns.

Indian pangolins are experts at this trick. They curl so tight that they look like a scaly pine cone. Some animals sniff them and just walk away!

WADDLE WALK

24

Thump thump! A pangolin waddles down a trail on its back legs.

Pangolins walk in a funny way. They stand up on their back legs and waddle. Their front paws curl under to keep their claws safe. Pangolins hold their tails off the ground for balance.

Some pangolins are great climbers too. They grip tree bark with their claws. Their strong tails wrap around branches like a hand.

The black-bellied pangolin is so at home in the trees that when it cannot reach the next branch, it stretches its long tail out to grab hold of it, then pulls itself across!

NIGHT SHIFT
DID YOU KNOW?
A pangolin can travel more
than a mile in just one night of
walking!

Hoot! An owl calls as a Sunda pangolin starts its nightly walk.

Pangolins are nocturnal. That means they are awake at night and sleep during the day. When the sky gets dark, they head out to find food.

A pangolin roams for hours each night. It covers a lot of ground. It never stays in one spot for very long.

Sunda pangolins start moving when the stars come out. They wander through the dark forest all night long. Then they find a safe place and rest until dark again.

SOLO STROLLERS

Shh! A lone pangolin slips quietly through the tall grass.

Pangolins like to be alone. They do not live in herds or packs. Each one roams its own part of the forest all by itself.

Pangolins mark their space with a strong smell from special glands near their tail. It's kind of like a skunk, but not quite as stinky! This warns other pangolins to keep out. Each pangolin knows where its space ends and another begins.

Being alone actually helps pangolins survive. Ant and termite nests are spread out across the forest, so there is usually only enough food for one hungry pangolin at a time.

FINDING
FRIENDS

Whiff! A male pangolin catches a female's smell on the breeze.

Pangolins find each other using smell. A male follows the scent of a female through the forest. When they meet, the two pangolins may bump noses or walk side by side. After a short while, the male leaves. He returns to living alone.

Pangolins usually mate in the spring. After they mate, the mother is on her own. She will raise her baby all by herself.

Male pangolins battle over females by swinging their heavy, scale-covered tails like clubs until one gives up.

PRECIOUS PANGOPUPS

Squeak! A baby pangolin is curled up safe in its burrow.

Most pangolins have one baby, but some Asian species can have up to three at a time. The tiny baby is called a pangopup. It is born with soft, pale scales that harden in a few days.

A newborn pangopup is very small. It weighs only a few ounces. Its eyes open soon after birth. The little pup can wiggle right away.

With its scales still soft, a newborn pangopup has no armor yet. That is why it stays hidden safe inside the burrow until its tough, protective scales grow in.

PIGGYBACK RIDES

Plop! A baby pangolin hops right onto its mother's wide tail.

Baby pangolins ride on their mothers. The little pangopup climbs onto the base of its mother's tail. It holds on tight as she walks through the forest.

The mother curls around her baby when danger is near. Her hard scales protect them both. She keeps her pangopup close for many months.

Mothers leave their babies in burrows for the first few weeks. Babies stay in the burrow while their mothers hunt at night.

After about two years, the pangopup is fully grown and ready to live on its own.

POACHING PROBLEMS

Crash! A spotlight shines, a pangolin runs for cover!

Pangolins are in big trouble. They are the most trafficked mammals on Earth. That means more pangolins are taken from the wild than any other mammal.

Some people hunt pangolins for their scales. Others hunt them for their meat. These people are called poachers.

Forests are being cut down too, which destroys their homes.

Chinese pangolins have lost many of their kind. All eight types of pangolins are now endangered. They need our help right away.

SAVING SCALES
38

Click! A vet checks a pangolin inside a rescue center.

People all over the world are working to save pangolins. Rescue centers take in hurt and lost pangolins. Vets help heal them.

New laws make it illegal to buy or sell pangolins. Rangers guard the forests where they live. Scientists attach tiny trackers to pangolins so they can follow them and learn where they go, what they eat, and how they live. Every new discovery helps people protect them even more.

FUN FACT!

World Pangolin Day is on the third Saturday of February every year!

GLOSSARY

Poachers
People who illegally hunt or capture wild animals.

Den
A safe spot where an animal rests or sleeps.

Keratin
The hard stuff that makes up scales and fingernails.

Endangered
An animal species with so few left in the wild that it could disappear forever.

Mammal
A warm-blooded animal that feeds its babies milk.